# YOUR KNOWLEDGE HAS VALUE

# Barriers to the use of an IT PMM in a large financial institution

**Bibliographic information published by the German National Library:**

The German National Library lists this publication in the National Bibliography; detailed bibliographic data are available on the Internet at http://dnb.dnb.de.

ISBN: 9783963555008
This book is also available as an ebook.

© GRIN Publishing GmbH
Trappentreustraße 1
80339 München

Print and binding: Books on Demand GmbH, Norderstedt, Germany
Printed on acid-free paper from responsible sources.

The present work has been carefully prepared. Nevertheless, authors and publishers do not incur liability for the correctness of information, notes, links and advice as well as any printing errors.

GRIN web shop: https://www.grin.com/document/1446237

# 'Barriers to the use of an IT PMM[1] in a large financial institution': a critical resume.

## Critical appraisal of a case study

Date:     20 December 2017

---

[1] Project Management Methodology

# Table of contents

## Introduction

During the early 2000s, it was argued that there was a need for ways to determine the quality of qualitative studies in medicine (Dixon-Woods M & Fitzpatrik R., 2001), and therefore, a need for developing appraisal criteria for qualitative research (Dixon-Woods et al.). Critically appraising journal articles allows one to filter out the low-quality studies and distinguish misleading information (Cormack, Gerrish & Lacey, 2010). In an attempt to apply this to the field of management, whilst reducing the possibility of flaws and classification errors, the CEBMa[2] adapted appraisal questionnaires for specific study designs (CEBMa, 2014), one of which – 'Appraisal of a Case Study' – shall act the basis of this critical essay (see Appendix H).

## Background

The article in review is featured in Elsevier's[3] International Journal of Project Management and was made available online on ScienceDirect.com[4] on the 8 of January 2016. As declared in the journal's 'Author Information Pack' document, "Papers by the editorial board are selected for publication based on their relevance, clarity, topicality, the extent to which they advance knowledge, and their contribution to inspiring further development and research" (IJPM, 2017). The information pack contains a strict and lengthy checklist of requirements and guidelines for researchers to adhere to, before submitting their research for publishing in the IJPM[5]. Hence, a

---

[2] Center for Evidence-Based Management
[3] Elsevier is an information and analytics company and one of the world's primary providers of scientific, technical, and medical information.
[4] ScienceDirect is a website which provides subscription-based access to a large database of scientific, technical and medical research.
[5] The International Journal of Project Management (IJPM) offers wide ranging and comprehensive coverage of all facets of project management.

journal article undergoes a rigorous test prior to being released and therefore, at face value, one can expect this study to be trustworthy and of adequate quality.

Authors, M.A. Terlizzi, F. de Souza Meirelles, and H.R.O.C. de Moraes researched under the auspices of the Sao Paolo School of Business Administration (Fundação Getulio Vargas), a Brazilian Higher Education institution. All three are Brazilian nationals and hold considerable experience in IT, IT Governance, Business Administration, Project Management and Academia (FGV EAESP, CNPq, 2017). The researchers did not comment on their own role and any professional bias they might have possibly caused. As emphasised by Coates (2011) "it is important that researchers are aware of their own preconceptions and strive to ensure that they do not allow them to bias their interpretation of the data".

The context is set in the introductory section (Appendix A, B) by the authors' reference to historical events in the financial sector (the global economic crisis of 2008), as well as developments (climate) in the banking industry at the time of writing (stringent regulation, use of IT governance and control mechanisms).

# Article assessment

## Title, abstract and keywords
The title of this article 'Barriers to the use of an IT PMM in a large financial institution' indicates the outcomes of the study. It can inform the reader of the research aim, however, it fails to mention that the research has been conducted within a specific geo-financial area, that is, Brazil. At first glance (or as the article shows up in search results) this could potentially mislead the reader into thinking that all the findings are applicable and transferable to other settings. One can sense this 'distortion' immediately upon reading the abstract where the context (Brazilian FSI[6]) is clearly stated. Here, the authors managed to condense and explain everything that is declared in the central text; the study rationale, aims, methodology and results. The five keywords pertaining to this article are faithful to the text and references; all are explored and given equal importance in the literature review (see Appendix D) having 'PMM',' PMS'[7] and 'IT Projects' as the overarching themes within the realm of 'IT Governance' in the 'Financial Service Industry'.

## Research question(s) and study design
Through their experience (FGV EAESP, CNPq, 2017) and market analysis, the researches aimed at addressing both the issues in the FSI (stakeholders were being affected from project failures), as well as gaps in research where emphasis on the need for exploratory research is made. The authors, referring to the Brazilian Financial Institutions, claim, "no study has attempted to determine whether implemented PMMs are properly used by these organisations."

---

[6] Financial service industry
[7] Project Management Success

5

*"To what degree is an IT PMM implemented in a large Brazilian financial institution? How is an implemented IT PMM that contributes to PMS used in a large Brazilian financial institution?"*

By posing the aforementioned research questions (rather exploratory and similar to 'how does it work?'), one is to expect explanation-type answers as outcomes from this study.

The article is well set out, permitting the research design to be effortlessly recognisable and easily read (Appendix D). According to CEBMa's 'Which Research Design for Which Question?' matrix (Appendix G), a case study design is deemed as an appropriate approach to tackle such questions. Single case research designs are sensitive to individual organism differences, and, as stated by Kazdin A. (1982), are used primarily to evaluate the effect of a variety of interventions in applied research. One has to keep in mind that a study design is never strong or weak in itself as it all depends on the question and the availability (EBMgt, 2017). Despite the fact that case studies rank at the lower levels on the 'Hierarchy of Evidence Pyramid' (Appendix F), a study design's strength rather depends on the question and the availability, as pointed out by Sackett and Wennberg (1997) - 'focusing on the question being asked is more important than squabbling over the "best" method'. Rychetnik et al. (2002) also state that 'the levels of the hierarchy are about the narrow concept of study design, and not the broader concept of evidence'.

**References, citations and search strategy**

Criteria establishing 'the best age' of evidence are quite varied – some suggest using "the current best evidence" or "the most current evidence", while others recommend having "all citations less than ten years old" (Shorten, 2013). 'Abundance of literature' was not an issue here, since the authors stated that there is "a lack of both qualitative and quantitative research" in the field. One could say that this could have driven them to rely mainly on older articles, but, his was not the case. Throughout the study, the authors cite older works primarily to demonstrate lasting concepts, else, to identify similar/identical outcomes from different studies across the years, as shown in the following extracts:

> *"These failures are surprising, given that the use of a PMM increases PMS rates (Atkinson, 1999; Baccarini, 1999; Tan, 2011; Thomas and Fernández, 2008; Wit, 1988), and PMMs are recommended for the Brazilian FSI."*

> *"Exploring the causes of a problem can enrich the understanding of a given theory and allow readers to make more sense of complex organisational phenomena (Whetten, 1989)."*

The illustration in 'Appendix E' is an attempt at assessing how relevant the citations are by sorting the references in a distribution according to their 'age'. One can observe that the majority have been published from the year 2000 onwards (that is, fifteen years, at most, before the date of publishing of the article). Interestingly, in a recent study conducted by Google Inc., it was found that by having easy access to older articles as much as recent ones, researchers now tend to cite the most relevant articles, regardless of their age (Versta et al., 2014). Another factor is "the dramatic growth in the number of articles published per-year, which has increased the number of recent articles that researchers need to situate their work in relation to by citing".

As for the task of searching for the related literature, publication characteristics are stated in the introductory part of the literature review:

> "...an analysis of the prior PMM literature is important to clarify IT governance and its role in relation to a PMM as well as the differences between the PS and PMS concepts".

This shows that the authors prioritised over other types of sources, however, failed to mention any specific research databases used, any publication biases, the way the search was conducted and whether any studies were rejected.

**Methodology, sample selection and collection of data**
Decisions need to be made continually throughout the research process (Willig, 2008); the research question, method of data collection and data analysis all depend on each other. Therefore it is of benefit to the reader to know about the determination of the research method.

Qualitative research looks at social phenomena, giving people the opportunity to understand what people do and why. Here, the researchers are trying to highlight the attitudes, experiences and emotions of participants concerning barriers to the use of project management methodology. The research does not use statistics, rather participant's responses and their subjective experiences around the topic.

Having managed to get access to organisational information, the researchers did their utmost to acquire quality data, for which collection methods were clearly described. In-depth interviews were conducted with the bank's Project Management Office experts, as well as four senior managers; the latter was done with the aim of building on the second question in the survey. In order to maximise on the extraction of data from the organisation's database, the authors had to understand project statuses to be able to apply strict selection criteria and review the best possible number of projects. Finally, the online software 'Survey Monkey' was used to send an electronic questionnaire. Via their exercise, the researchers gathered hard data (project details and success rates) as well as soft data (perceptions on the use of PMM from employees as well as additional feedback).

Although not systematic (in research terms), the article demonstrates that the researchers retrieved evidence in an orderly manner. The research methodology may lead to the suggestion that the participants were selected using purposive convenience sampling, most commonly used in large-scale studies (Sim & Wright, 2000). Although very useful to researchers in situations where a targeted sample needs to be reached quickly, the use of convenience sampling may mean that subjects were not the most appropriate to the task (Burnard & Newell, 2011). In this case, the researchers relied on professional experience, and all the 'handpicked' subjects consisted of:

- IT Professionals with 'Project Manager' roles
- Senior Managers with more than five years of experience as project managers' responsible for relevant IT projects, and
- 3047 projects initiated after June 30, 2014, with both initiating and planning phase status 'concluded' (as specified in the company's database)

The authors give no explanation as to why the participants chose to take part in the electronic questionnaire or why others declined. Such information would be essential as there may be a specific group of people who are willing to participate in research studies, and therefore the research might not be generalisable for the entire organisation.

**Analysis and results**

Results, which consisted mainly of qualitative feedback, are deemed to be credible since they resonate with the literature and expected outcomes, however, the study was "specifically used to understand the organization's shortcomings and to develop an action plan", hence making it relevant to the organisation in question. The authors state that "analysis of documentation and interviews was carried out specialist staff", "each interview was transcribed and read several times" and "comments analysed individually"; however one cannot tell whether this analysis was repeated by more than one researcher. The conclusions drawn were reviewed by the stakeholders, who, "at the end of the study developed a new IT PMM for small projects", and other quality processes became mandatory. This implies that stakeholders agreed that conclusions drawn were justified by the results.

### Ethics

Although no names have been mentioned throughout the article, there might be ethical issues relating to the welfare of participants, such as the certain comments which disclosed employee-sensitive information (ex. "I am blind, and the project management tool is not accessible for use with the screen reader's software; for this reason, I cannot work as a project manager."). The article does not mention approval by any ethics entity, but, given that this was an organisation-based collaborative research, one can presume that each questionnaire and interview participant volunteered for this study, and that informed consent was gained.

## Transferability to other settings

As stated in the 'Strengths and Limitations' section, this journal article is representative of one company in Brazil, but its outcomes (although not generalisable) could be beneficial for IT Project Managers or other stakeholders in the Financial Services Industries across the globe. There is a short time period between the article being written (mid-2015) and it being published (beginning of 2016) (see Appendix B), which means that the information presented could be deemed relevant and up to date. Nonetheless, one cannot be confident in saying that this study is transferable to other settings. One cannot tell whether both the setting and the subjects are representative with regard to the Banking Industry in general; the setting (worldwide organisation) is representative, however, the subjects (IT professionals) are not.

## Concluding remarks

Overall, the authors have demonstrated that critical thinking was applied and that the best available evidence was taken into consideration. The use of the English language is commendable, in that, any elaborate literature and concepts were simplified. The researchers successfully adopted the process of evidence-based practice (Barends et. al, 2014) in order to achieve the desired outcomes, that is, they: 'Asked' - the issues and gaps present were translated into two answerable questions; 'Acquired' - the researcher searched for and retrieved evidence pertaining to PMM and PMS in an orderly manner via the literature review, surveys and interviews; 'Appraised' - subsequently, judgement on the trustworthiness and relevance of the evidence was exercised; 'Aggregated' - everything (literature, research results etc.) was aggregated into a single embedded case study; 'Applied' - incorporated evidence from literature and other findings to one organisation into the research process as well as proposed an action plan; 'Assessed' - evaluated the outcome from the research. The researchers themselves have identified quite a number of limitations, allowing others to possibly replicate the study. Nonetheless, the reader is advised to take into consideration the non-declaration of biases and other crucial 'shortages' mentioned in this review before citing this case study.

# References

Barends, E., Rousseau, D., & Briner, R. (2014). *Evidence-Based Management: The Basic Principles.* Amsterdam, The Netherlands: Center for Evidence-Based Management.

Berman, S. (2007, March). Review: Case Studies and Theory Development in the Social Sciences by Alexander L. George and Andrew Bennett. *Perspectives on Politics , 5 (1) ,* 187-188. American Political Science Association.

CEBMa. (2014, July). *Critical Appraisal Checklist for a Case Study.* Retrieved October 28, 2017, from www.cebma.org: https://www.cebma.org/resources-and-tools/what-is-critical-appraisal/

CEBMa. (n.d.). *What are the levels of evidence?* Retrieved December 13, 2017, from CEBMa.org: https://www.cebma.org/faq/what-are-the-levels-of-evidence/

CNPq. (n.d.). *Heverton Roberto Oliveira Cesar de Moraes.* Retrieved December 10, 2017, from lattes.cnpq.br: http://buscatextual.cnpq.br/buscatextual/visualizacv.do?id=K4339219T3&idiomaExibicao=2

CNPq. (n.d.). *Marco Alexandre Terlizzi.* Retrieved December 10, 2017, from http://lattes.cnpq.br/: http://buscatextual.cnpq.br/buscatextual/visualizacv.do?id=K4302185Z9&idiomaExibicao=2

Coates, V. (2011). Research and diabetes nursing. *Journal of Diabetes Nursing , 15* (4), 142-148.

Dixon-Woods, M., Shaw, R., Agarwal, S., & Smith, J. (2004). The problem of appraising qualitative research. *BMJ Quality & Safety , 13* (3), 223-225.

FGV EAESP. (n.d.). *Fernando De Souza Meirelles.* Retrieved December 10, 2017, from eaesp.fgv.br: eaesp.fgv.br/professores

Gerrish, K., & Lacey, A. (2010). *The research process in nursing.* Chichester, West Sussex, U.K. Ames, Iowa: Wiley-Blackwell.

Gibbert, M., & Ruigrok, W. (2010). The "What and "How" of Case Study Rigor: Three Strategies Based on Published Work. *Organizational Research Methods , 13* (4), 710-737.

Gibbert, M., Ruigrok, W., & Wicki, B. (2008). What passes as a rigorous case study? *Strategic Management Journal , 29* (13), 1465-1474.

I.J.P.M. (n.d.). *Author Information Pack.* Retrieved December 1, 2017, from Elsevier.com: www.elsevier.com/locate/ijproman: https://www.elsevier.com/wps/find/journaldescription.cws_home/30435?generatepdf=true

Kazdin, A. (1982). *Single-Case Research Designs.* New York: Oxford University Press.

Newell, R., & Burnard, P. *Research for evidence-based practice in healthcare.* Chichester, West Sussex, UK Ames, Iowa: Wiley-Blackwell.

Petticrew, M., & Roberts, H. (2003). Evidence, hierarchies, and typologies: horses for courses. *Journal of Epidemiology & Community Health , 57,* 527-529.

13

Rychetnik, L., Frommer, M., Hawe, P., & Shiell, A. (2002). Criteria for evaluating evidence on public health interventions. *Journal of Epidemiology & Community Health , 56*, 119-127.

Sackett, D., & Wennberg, J. (1997). Choosing the best research design for each question. *British Medical Journal , 315* (7123), 1636.

Shorten, D. (2013, September 26). *When is the evidence too old?* Retrieved December 13, 2017, from Evidence-Based Nursing blog: http://blogs.bmj.com/ebn/2013/09/26/when-is-the-evidence-too-old/

Siggelkow, N. (2007). Persusasion with Case Studies. *The Academy of Management Journal , 50* (1), 20-24.

Sim, J., & Wright, C. (2000). *Research in health care: concepts, designs and methods.* Cheltenham: Thornes Ltd.

Terlizzi, M. A., de Souza Meirelles, F., & de Moraes, R. H. (2016). Barriers to the use of an IT Project Management Methodology in a large financial institution. *International Journal of Project Management* (34(3)), 467-479.

Verstak, A., Acharya, A., Suzuki, H., Henderson, S., Iakhiaev, M., Lin, C., et al. (2014, November 4). *On the Shoulders of Giants: The Growing Impact of Older Articles.* Retrieved December 5, 2017, from scholar.googleblog.com: https://arxiv.org/pdf/1411.0275.pdf

Willig, C. (2008). *Introducing Qualitative Research In Psychology.* Open University Press.

# YOUR KNOWLEDGE HAS VALUE